The Entrepreneur-Mindset
Get up! Get out! Be awesome!

by Stefan F.M. Dittrich

Bibliografische Information der Deutschen Nationalbibliothek: Die Deutsche Nationalbibliothek verzeichnet diese Publikation in der Deutschen Nationalbibliografie; detaillierte bibliografische Daten sind im Internet über http://dnb.dnb.de/ abrufbar.

www.master-mindset.com

Herstellung und Verlag: BoD – Books on Demand, Norderstedt

ISBN-13: 9-783744-899642

Stefan F.M. Dittrich, born and raised in Germany, graduated from Personal- and Business-Coaching and passed a qualified vocational Training in the field of NLP. He is a great Supporter of "Lean StartUp" or "Lean Management" (see also Eric Ries or Ash Maurya) but also takes the Position that a great StartUp is based on the Entrepreneurs Personality and Mindset.

As a well educated Personal- and Business-Coach Stefan Dittrich is helping Managers and Employees reflecting Strategies, Processes and Habits. He also is experienced as an Entrepreneur, Trainer and Team-Leader.

Table of Content

Synopsis   1

How to Use This Book?   3

In this Book you'll learn…   4

Do You Have an Entrepreneurial Mindset – A Quiz   6

Which One Are You?   8

Do you base your life-style on your revenue?   9

Let's look at some more differences!   10

What Is An Entrepreneurial Mindset And Why Is It   13
Important?

The two kinds of mindsets   17

What Does Changing Your Mind Mean?   18

How to Change Your Mind in Order to Change Your   20
Life

Do You Use Procrastination as a Way to Avoid   23
Perfectionism?

Do You View a Challenge as Fearful?   24

Focus on the Process and not on the Praise   25

Developing a Positive Attitude   26

The Motivation Equation   32

How to Generate a Steady Stream of Ideas   37

How to Engage Your Creative Problem Solving Brain   38

How to Be More Open and Aware Of Opportunities   40

Take Advantage of Your Resources   44

How to Wear the Entrepreneurial Hat   49

How to Share Your Business Vision   54

How to Be a Problem Solver   57

Entrepreneurial Mindset Means Being Willing To Take Risks   61

Entrepreneurs Always Learn and Improve   64

Entrepreneurs Know Their Strengths and Weaknesses   67

Entrepreneurs Live a Balanced Life   69

A Positive Mindset and Productivity   71

Learn To Listen to Customers!   77

Be A Good Provider!   81

Find A Mentor and Coaching!   85

About the Master-Mindset Method   94

Introduction

Synopsis

Many small business owners and enterprisers got their beginning as an employee. They worked for somebody else. The issue is, if you've been an employee for years, it may be difficult to shake of the bonds of the employee mentality.

What does this mean?

If you've an employee mentality, you're more likely to look to other people to tell you what to do. You'll find it difficult to take responsibility for the success and failure of your endeavor.

You see, as an employee, you've no say about how the business is executed. You just work hard to prove your value so that you can stay employed.

There are a lot of employees who are longing to be their own boss, yet are fearsome of what the future may hold if they were business owners. I would like to advise that if you're among those individuals, you'd do well to become a great employee first! I spent a lot of years as an employee and was constantly found to be a model employee.

My entrepreneur bosses constantly gave me high evaluations. In going over the list of employee mentalities, I can frankly tell you that I didn't have those mentalities. I was a great employee!

If you have a want to be on your own one day, going after your dreams as an entrepreneur, you are able to begin now. Approach your occupation as though you owned the company where you work. Bearing that ownership spirit will reward you on the job and ready you for the day when you are able to pursue your own business. You are able to be an entrepreneur while you're still working. Having this spirit will excite you to go after your own endeavors when you're not on your employer's time clock.

How to Use This Book?

This Book is designed to help you develop and embrace an entrepreneurial spirit and mindset. Use the information provided over the next 20 pages to fine tune the areas where your entrepreneurial mindset may need a little work. It's okay if you need to work on all areas. Mindset is learned, not engrained in your DNA.

The path of business ownership and creation is one filled with continuous learning, adaptation, and growth. Developing your entrepreneurial mindset is part of that path and process.

There are two potential approaches to using this Book:

The first is to read it through cover to cover. Then go back and review and work on the areas where you need the most improvement. Or work on the areas that inspire you. This is the appropriate approach if you like to read material and think on it before you take action. However, you may want to keep a notBook handy when you're reading so you can jot down any thoughts or notes.

The second approach is to read the Book and take action as you work your way through it. For example, if you are inspired and motivated to start working on your ability to visualize then take action on that inspiration.

Of course you can always take a combined approach. Take notes on some items and action on others!

At the core of any entrepreneur is someone who is so excited and passionate about their business that they're ready willing and able to take risks. They're positive about the direction they're headed and they're willing to bring others along for the ride – in fact they'd prefer it that way.

It's about being more than a business owner – you're a problem solver and a creator. You're an entrepreneur!

In this Book you'll learn:

- How to get and stay positive
- How to get and stay motivated

- How to generate a steady stream of ideas – tapping into your creative side
- How to be more open and aware of opportunities
- How to consistently take advantage of your resources
- How to wear the entrepreneurial hat (you're more than a manager)
- How to share your business vision
- How to be a problem solver
- How to take more risk – confidently
- How to create a plan for lifelong learning and self improvement
- How to become more self aware - know your strengths and weaknesses
- How to live a balanced life

Let's get started with a little quiz:

Do You Have an Entrepreneurial Mindset – A Quiz

Simply answer yes or no to the following 15 questions. The more yes answers you have, the stronger your entrepreneurial mindset.

- I passionately seek new opportunities.

- I am focused and determined.

- I effectively tune out negative people, comments and thoughts.

- I am confident in business.

- I take inspired action and make decisions quickly

- I regularly see opportunities around me

- I have many fulfilling business relationships

- I enjoy sharing my vision with others

- I take advantage of my resources

- I am creative and/or enjoy creative problem solving.

- I am comfortable making tough choices.

- I know my strengths and weaknesses

- I trust my gut.

- I know when something isn't working for me.

- I'm not afraid to fail.

How many Yes answers did you have? _____

Don't worry if you have zero yes answers. That's what this Book is for! Take the quiz at the end of the Book, after you have worked on the entrepreneurial attributes discussed in this Book, go back and take the quiz again.

Which One Are You?

If you're an entrepreneur or business owner, you think much differently. Essentially the buck stops (and begins) with you. You're responsible for the success and failure of your endeavor. And you are the one who makes all the huge decisions (including who to designate littler decisions to!).

To discover if you're actual own thinking, please take a moment and think about the following questions:

- Do you confine your tasks/responsibilities to a subset of what is required for your business to flourish?

- Do you base your life-style on your revenue?

- If a money setback happens, do you shrink your budget to adapt to the reduction in revenue?

- Do you constantly seek outside advice to make even daily decisions?

If you responded "yes" to most of these queries, chances are you've an employee mentality. Here's why those with an entrepreneur mentality would answer "no."

Do you confine your tasks/responsibilities to a subset of what is required for your business to flourish?

Entrepreneurs understand that occasionally they have to do things in their business that are "higher up" or "beneath" their skill level. Their mental attitude is if it has to get accomplished, get it accomplished and they're not adverse to bundling up their sleeves and getting their arms dirty.

Do you base your life-style on your revenue?

Entrepreneurs will seek to develop their business, enlarge their line of products and broaden their services when money setbacks happen. They don't let themselves get to be or remain a victim of fiscal conditions. If a money setback happens, do you shrink your budget to accommodate the reduction in revenue?

Entrepreneurs send out the payments for themselves first. They center on bringing in the money that supports the life-style they want and invest the rest into their business. That stated, they're likewise cognizant of and accept the fleeting sacrifices that may need to be made in order to achieve a goal.

Do you constantly seek outside advice to make even daily decisions?

Entrepreneurs handle their time and take responsibility for their actions. While they might seek out mentors to guide them to expanded growth, they're in control of their day-to-day actions and don't need somebody else to tell them what to accomplish or prompt them to accomplish it.

Let's look at some more differences!

Monday mentality:

- Employees fear Monday. (Or, whatever the beginning day of their work week is.)

- Entrepreneurs are not bolted into a work week. They approach each day as a different chance to go after their dreams.

It's not my problem mentality:

- Employees have this mentality they view everything on the job by whether or not it's their problem.

- Entrepreneurs view everything as their duty as they have ownership of what is happening in their business.

T. G. I. F. (Thank Goodness It's Friday) mentality:

- Employees are constantly looking forward to their off days.

- Entrepreneurs are forever seeking ways to extend their business even when they're not "working" they're considering ways to extend their entrepreneurial talents. They look forward to each day!

"When am I going to receive a raise?"-mentality:

- Employees think that raises ought to come according to the calendar, instead of according to their work.

- Entrepreneurs seldom consider when they'll receive an increase. They realize that the more they work towards helping other people the greater their reward will be.

"Oh no, what now?"-mentality:

- Employees set about meetings with an "oh no" mentality.

- Entrepreneurs set about meetings with a mastermind mentality. They realize that excellent ideas come out of these meetings.

There are a lot more mindsets that we may compare. As a matter of fact if a few have come to mind for you as you read this, write them down!

What Is An Entrepreneurial Mindset And Why Is It Important?

There's a difference between being a business owner and being an entrepreneur. There are millions of business owners around the globe. There are much fewer entrepreneurs.

Why?

Being an entrepreneur requires a certain mindset. It's a mindset that many are born with. You've met and likely heard of people who have always had one business idea or another and acted on them regularly. From the time they were small children they were out making money and starting businesses.

These people were born with an entrepreneurial mindset. They are innovative, action takers who aren't afraid to make mistakes. They're also often very skilled at getting people to buy into their vision.

As a business owner, or aspiring business owner, you can benefit from this entrepreneurial mindset. You can grow your business well beyond your original plan and have a lot of fun along the way.

You see, entrepreneurs are:

1. Positive
2. Motivated
3. Innovative and creative
4. Open minded
5. Resourceful
6. Visionaries
7. Delegators
8. Problem solvers
9. Risk takers
10. Lifelong learners
11. Self aware
12. Balanced

These are the 12 key ingredients of an entrepreneurial mindset. Taking a look at the list it's not hard to see why an entrepreneurial mindset is so powerful in business. Chances are you already possess some of these key attributes. You may possess many of them in varying degrees.

For example, some days you're confident to take calculated risks. Other days, not so much. This Book is designed to help you cultivate all of these attributes – it's designed to help you develop and embrace an entrepreneurial mindset.

To put it quite simply, an entrepreneurial mindset gives you the power to:

- Recognize and capitalize on opportunities

- Operate from a place of confidence and courage

- Take calculated risks

- Stay passionate and enthusiastic

- Connect with, and lead, people who can help your business thrive and prosper

- Tap into the courage and determination it takes to make it through challenges

- Learn from, and capitalize on mistakes.

- Make an impact on your audience and in your world

Chapter One

The two kinds of mindsets

When it comes to mindsets, there are two kinds – a fixed mindset and a growth mindset. Changing your mind may be viewed as a negative; however, such is not the case. Changing your mind does not mean:

- You cannot make up your mind
- You are indecisive
- You are out of integrity and don't do what you say you will
- You are flighty
- You are unintelligent

Changing your mind, if you will, can assist you in creating a new life. You can change your mind in a positive way.

What Does Changing Your Mind Mean?

In the world of intelligence, learning, and academics, it means to have a new understanding. That understanding highlights an important psychological factor. When you take on something new, your brain records this new learning endeavor came about because you have expanded yourself, worked hard and learned something new. There is now a new connection for your brain to recall, which, over time, can actually make you smarter.

You have exercised your brain away from the thought that intelligence is static and that it is a growth process. The more you learn, the more you exercise your brain, the more you grow; therefore, the more you are capable of learning.

In the world of the everyday, have you ever noticed how one negative thing in your early morning routine (such as losing your car keys or spilling your coffee) has the power to set the tone of the entire rest of your day? Does your day continue to spiral downward into a negative cyclone of mishaps and misfortunes the more you focus on that one thing which started your day off poorly?

The next time that happens, take a moment to change your mind. It takes a challenge and plenty of practice, but it is so worth every minute of effort. Exercise your brain. Just like anything else, practice makes perfection. Take a moment to recognize that you are not the only one that things like this happen to. Hundreds of thousands of people around the globe have lost their car keys and spilled their coffee. They just don't let it ruin the rest of their day. Moreover, they don't let it rule the rest of their day.

Change your mind. Maybe you needed to run late this particular day because you were going to meet your next big client or the love of your life on the train that day. Perhaps you needed to avoid a big accident. Change your mind and change your life.

The same goes for learning new things. With a growth mindset, you can train your brain to view learning new subjects as a positive experience rather than a negative one.

How to Change Your Mind in Order to Change Your Life

Take some time to evaluate your own points of view. Don't hold back; be completely honest with yourself. Do you have a more negative outlook on life? Do you even get annoyed in the company of others who take on a more positive attitude? Are you so set in your ways, you are unwilling to explore, learn, and re-create your life?

If, you've answered yes to any of these pertinent questions, then there is one more question to ask. Do you wish to take responsibility for using your mindset and do the work to create the most growth you could ever have imagined or hoped for in all areas of your life? Once you have examined your views and thought patterns and beliefs in total honesty, you are ready to move on to the next step.

- Is a challenge simply an excuse to quit?
- Is a roadblock a way to host a pity party?
- Do you procrastinate in order to turn away from perfectionism?

- When someone else experiences success, do you feel less than?
- Do you view a challenge as something fearful?

Are You Willing to be Open to Something New?

What if you could take a good hard look at those questions and re-create them to show up as positives? Are you willing to be open to explore new possibilities? Transformation is yours if you are willing to do the work and walk the walk. With practice, any new way of being becomes a habit. It's your choice whether you want to have a habit of positive growth or negative decline.

Let's look at how this could potentially work.

A Challenge is a Form of Growth and not an Excuse to Quit

When faced with a challenge, it is easy to spend time and energy focusing on the challenge itself. The thoughts you think, such as it being too hard or why does this happen to me (also known as "woe is me" syndrome) can easily distract your energy from the task at hand. What would happen if you viewed your challenge as a way to grow and expand?

What if that new responsibility led to more money, a higher position, or a transfer with a promotion? This is how to view your situation from a growth mindset point of view.

Is a Roadblock a Chance to Host a Pity Party?

If you have a deep subconscious belief that "everything bad" happens to you, then the chances are high that you invite roadblocks into your life. Sometimes it's easier to host a pity party than to come up with creative and intelligent resources to solve the problem at hand. What would happen if you viewed a roadblock as an opportunity to use your creativity go around it or under it?

In a growth mindset, this is what you would take on – viewing a roadblock as a way to stretch, grow, and improve rather than something to feel sorry for yourself about and an excuse to quit.

Do You Use Procrastination as a Way to Avoid Perfectionism?

Does the thought of not being good enough haunt you, so you procrastinate? What would happen if you were to approach a project or a challenge as an opportunity to expand your horizons or to re-create yourself as a master at the task at hand? A growth mindset will offer you the opportunity to change your perception, face the task head-on, and take it on with all the vim and vigor you could ever desire.

When Someone Else Experiences Success, Do You Feel Less Than?

If someone else experiences success, you have a choice. Either you can be happy for them and inspired by them, making you want to strive higher, or you can feel resentful or jealous. Many people choose to allow the success of others make them feel bad about themselves. However, it does not have to be that way.

Individuals with a growth mindset hold the belief that intelligence can be learned and developed and it is not just for the elite few. It is available to anyone with a desire to improve. The brain is trainable.

Do You View a Challenge as Fearful?

When faced with a challenge do you become overwhelmed and debilitated by fear or do you grasp on tight and face it head on? Your mindset will determine how you handle a challenge and ultimately what the outcome of that challenge will be, as well.

People with a growth mindset know that a challenge is way of doing things differently, thinking smarter and working harder.

Focus on the Process and not on the Praise

As a parent, are you tempted to praise your child for every success both big and small? If you look at a new way of fostering a growth mindset, you will discover that praising the process is more effective. When your child figures something out and does a job well done, encourage and praise how, when and where they figured it out rather than the end goal itself. This encourages learning and growing and teaches children how to come up with creative and intelligent solutions rather than focusing only on the end goal.

Use Constructive Criticism

Criticism of any kind is thought of in a fixed mindset way, as though it is negative. However, constructive criticism offers a new model and method of teaching by showing what doesn't work and questioning what will work. By offering constructive criticism, it gives them the opportunity to figure out how to fix something in a positive light.

Chapter Two

Developing a Positive Attitude

Your mindset is the single most important definer of success. If you're positive about your business, where it's headed and your role in the creation and growth of it then you're in a great place. From that place of positive emotion anything can and will happen.

That being said, it can be difficult to sustain a positive attitude. Everyone has moment where negative thoughts, people, and emotions sneak in. The goal is to be able to recognize these moments, acknowledge them for what they are, and let them go. Here's how to develop and sustain a positive attitude.

#1 Passion

Passion and a positive attitude are directly linked. When you have passion for your business everything else falls in line much more easily. Unfortunately, you cannot develop passion for your business. You either have it or you do not. Hopefully, when you started your business it was something that you felt very strongly about.

If not, if you've never had passion for your business consider starting a business that you are passionate about. Learn from this and move forward.

Now, passion can wane. It can come and go. The secret to sustaining passion for your business is actually intricately linked with an entrepreneurial mindset. When you're looking for ways to grow and improve your business, passion grows with the activity, the changes and the opportunities you pursue.

#2 Create a Success Habit

 When you are able to consistently set goals and achieve them, you'll create a pattern of success. Success of course feels great. It helps you stay focused on what you can do, what you do well, and where you want to go. That's the essence of a positive mindset.

Not sure where to start? Create a realistic but motivating goal – a goal that you feel very good about. Create a series of smaller goals to help you achieve your big goal. Plan how you're going to achieve each smaller goal. As you succeed with each smaller goal, take a moment to celebrate the success.

#3 Acknowledge, Assess, and Release

Doubts, fears and negative thought can sneak in. No one is positive all the time. When you have moments of doubt, fear and negative thoughts recognize the emotion. Assess where it is coming from and why it is occurring. It may take some time if you're prone to negative thoughts and limiting beliefs.

What's a limiting belief?

Here are a few common examples,

- "This is never going to work."

- "I am such a terrible ____"

- "I'm bad with _____"

- "The only way to succeed is with luck."

- "I always mess this up."

If you frequently experience thoughts like these then it's vitally important to spend some time refocusing your thoughts. Think about what you do well. Examine where the negative thoughts are coming from and why they occur. Assess whether they're really true and what you can do about them.

#4 Positive Affirmations

We all struggle with limiting beliefs and doubts. You can turn these fears, limiting beliefs and doubts into positive affirmations. For example, "I am bad at writing" can turn into "I am a good communicator. I know my strengths and weaknesses and am wise enough to delegate and focus on my strengths."

Repeat the affirmation each time negativity seeps into your thoughts. Make a habit of repeating the positive affirmation regularly. Make it part of your inner dialogue.

#5 Visualization

Visualization is a powerful tool. It not only helps you foresee potential obstacles to success, it helps you feel successful and positive about your actions. Visualization, like most things, is a skill. Some people are born with exceptional visualization skills; however most of us can use some improvement.

When you're beginning to use visualization, you will likely begin by simply seeing what is happening in your imagination. However, adding your senses will not only enhance the experience, it will amplify the results. Sight, touch, smell, taste and hearing can all be integrated into your visualizations.

Practice visualization. The better you become at visualization the faster you will achieve success. You'll be better able to tap into positive thoughts, feelings and a sense of success and achievement. When you're feeling negatively, sit down and visualize success. It will become part of your DNA if you embrace positive thoughts on such a deep level.

#6 Surround Yourself with Positive People

The people in your life can play a very critical role in your attitude. Surrounded by negative people and naysayers? Consider asking them for support. Consider also finding a mentor, coach or mastermind group to help you stay focused and positive. Let go of the people in your life who cannot or will not support you.

Embrace those who support you and share the same outlook. That doesn't mean you surround yourself with "yes men." You don't need people who simply agree with you. Instead look for those who are also positive, motivated and share the same vision.

A positive outlook and motivation are intricately linked. You cannot feel motivated if you also don't feel good about what you're doing and where you're going.

Chapter Three

The Motivation Equation

Do you wake up each day excited to work on your business? Do you spend time thinking about your business even when you're not at work? For many, motivation is difficult to sustain. Some days are better than other. However, when you're truly excited about your business, and it becomes an active and positive part of your life, everything changes.

When you wake up each day and you feel motivated and excited about your business, it opens the door for the other aspects of an entrepreneurial mindset. You look for opportunities, you seize challenges, find creative solutions for problems and you effectively share your vision with others.

When you're not motivated it becomes difficult to do anything other than manage your business. And you're not a manager – you're an entrepreneur!

Let's take a look at a few key steps you can take to find motivation for your business. Note: If you can't summon any motivation for your present business, consider finding an idea that does inspire and motivate you.

#1 Gratitude

Gratitude is the ability to recognize and appreciate what you have. It's also a practice. How often do you feel gratitude? Do you feel appreciative of:

- The things you have?

- The people in your life?

- Your daily experiences?

Gratitude accomplishes amazing things. It helps you stay positive and it has a dramatic affect on your motivation. Why? Because gratitude is something you want to feel more of and you want others to feel. It permeates your spirit and becomes part of who you are.

In order to benefit from gratitude it's important to make it a part of your life. Consider creating a habit of gratitude. Start saying, and feeling, "Thank you" when you experience something wonderful or receive something in your life. Start acknowledging the things you are grateful for. You can journal or simply create a daily practice of mentally listing the things you're grateful for.

#2 Focus On Your Strengths and Joyous and Fulfilling Activities

What do you love to do? What are you good at?

Don't know? Make a list. Start with the activities you love to do and the topics you're passionate about.

Then create a plan to integrate these joyous and fulfilling activities into your day. Make sure you do something you love each and every day. It is sure to get you out of bed in the morning and excited and motivated for your day.

#3 Celebrate

Celebrate your successes. Each day, whatever you accomplish it doesn't matter if it is big or small, celebrate your successes. It'll add a smile to your face, a bounce to your step, and it will help you stay motivated to achieve more success.

#4 Get Inspired

One great way to stay inspired and motivated is to surround yourself with inspiration. So what inspires you? Music? Art? Books?

Create a home office that you enjoy spending time in. Surround yourself with the things you love. And of course, take the time to surround yourself with inspiring people.

It's hard to feel unmotivated with such greatness all around you.

#5 Take Breaks

An annual vacation isn't enough. It's very important to your mental health and wellbeing to take breaks. Schedule daily breaks. Make sure to take time off weekly and monthly. And of course don't forget those annual vacations if that's part of your tradition.

Even a few hours or a day or two can really make a difference. It gives you time to recharge and find that original source of inspiration and motivation.

Motivation can wane from day to day and even from task to task. However, being able to sustain motivation for your business is important. You want to feel excited about you business. It's the only way to really make it grow. Speaking of growth, the next step is all about tapping into your creative side and generating great, not to mention profitable, business ideas.

Chapter Four

How to Generate a Steady Stream of Ideas – Tapping Into Your Creative Side

How innovative are you? Are you able to consistently practice creative brainstorming? Do you enjoy the process?

Many people don't consider themselves to be "Creative types" yet everyone has the potential to be creative. Additionally, being creative doesn't mean you have to paint, write poetry or play a musical instrument. You can, sure, but it's not required.

Instead think of begin creative as:

- Innovation

- Out of the box thinking

- Problem solving

Creative thinking means pondering the possibilities of what could be, without restrictions based on what is.

You might brainstorm:

- A new perspective on how to perform a task.

- A new way to market your business.

- A new partnership or joint venture.

- A new product or service.

How to Engage Your Creative Problem Solving Brain

Identify two or three problems your business is facing. They might be systems, strategies or even products or services.

Once you have your problems listed, brainstorm solutions. Write them down. Think about solutions without limiting yourself. Whenever a doubt surfaces about a potential solution push it aside.

Focus solely on brainstorming possibilities without restrictions or limitations. Push yourself to come up with potential solutions. This will really challenge you to get creative with your answers.

Consider doing something routine while you're brainstorming. For example, toss a ball from hand to hand. Chop vegetables or some other activity that requires eye and hand coordination. Studies have shown that this practice opens up another area of your brain.

It's why great ideas come to us when we're driving, exercising and other routine activities. Try it if you have trouble tapping into your creative side.

Add creative brainstorming sessions into your regular work week. Make it part of your life as an entrepreneur. It's a part of your work week you'll begin to look forward to and it'll generate amazing results.

In addition to brainstorming ideas and opportunities it's important to be aware of the opportunities already present in your life. Chapter Five talks about how to be more open and aware of opportunities.

Chapter Five

How to Be More Open and Aware Of Opportunities

Every day new opportunities come your way. The problem is that most people don't recognize them. And those that do recognize the opportunity let fear, doubt and negativity get in the way of taking action.

This is why so many of these entrepreneurial mindset elements are important. Right away you can see that staying positive helps you take action and recognize opportunities. They're all linked together – strengthen one and you strengthen them all.

There are essentially five steps to be more open to opportunities that come your way.

Step #1 Stay Positive

If you're feeling negative then your head is down and you're focusing on limitations. It's the opposite of what you want to do. Stay positive and expect good things. You'll recognize them when they come your way. Refer back to Chapter One on how to get and stay positive.

Step #2 Listen

There's a lot going on in your community, both online and off. Listen to what your community is saying. Pay attention to leaders in your industry. Listen to your customers and listen to those around you. Sometimes listening is difficult. We get involved in talking, sharing and making a great impression. Try listening to those around you instead of talking and see what happens.

Step #3 Be Open Minded

It's easy to shut the door on an opportunity. It takes an open mind to consider all the possibilities that come your way. An open mind often requires courage and a positive attitude – two other qualities of an entrepreneurial mindset.

Step #4 Take Inspired Action

You might be the kind of person that regularly recognizes opportunities. However, do you then take action on those that come your way? Action doesn't mean diving headlong into a new commitment. Instead, action might be as simple as brainstorming ideas related to the opportunity or researching it further.

It's not enough to acknowledge an opportunity. See an opportunity and take action! It's one of the core components of an entrepreneurial mindset.

Step #5 Look for Opportunities

Finally, and this is an integral part of the "Creative Thinking" attribute that has already been discussed, start looking for opportunities. It's not enough to wait for them to come your way. Start looking for opportunities or making them for yourself.

Now, we just talked about taking inspired action. That can be difficult if you're not taking advantage of all your resources. You can't do everything yourself!

Chapter Six

Take Advantage of Your Resources

Entrepreneurs know two very important things.

1. They know they cannot, and should not, do it all.

2. They know that others can and are willing to help - they use their resources

What Are Your Resources?

Take a look around you and make a list of your resources. Consider:

- The people in your life

- The people you can bring into your life (for example, contractors, consultants and mentors)

- The technology in your life

- The technology you can bring into your life

- Your skills, knowledge and abilities

- The skills, knowledge and abilities of others

- Financial assets

The list could go on and on because resources are all around you.

Unfortunately, many business owners get into the mindset that they have to do it all. They have to be the manager, sales person, customer service department, financial officer, and so on. It leaves very little, if any, time for the "entrepreneur."

If you're always taking care of the business, how do you grow it?

Easy – You grow it by taking advantage of your resources.

Step #1 Identify Your Resources.

Who and what do you have in your life right now that can help you with your business? For example, do you have technology that you're not taking advantage of that can simplify some of your systems? Do you know a bookkeeper that could manage your accounting so you don't have to?

Step #2 Identify Where You Need Help Right Now

Spend some time looking at where you need help. What tasks are you managing that:

- Take up too much time

- Aren't enjoyable

- Don't match your skill set

- Don't result in direct profits

These are prime opportunities to take advantage of your resources. Additionally, if you don't have a resource to solve a problem go out and get one.

For example, if you need someone to take over your bookkeeping but you don't know a bookkeeper then hire a bookkeeper. Your time is too valuable to spend it on tasks that "manage" your business. You need time to be the entrepreneur.

Step #3 Acknowledge Future Opportunities as Potential Resources

You just never know when you're going to be presented with a potential solution. And these solutions often pop up when you don't need them.

For example, you're in line at the grocery store and you start a conversation with the person in line ahead of you. You quickly learn that they're a graphic designer. You don't have a need for a graphic designer so you nod politely.

A month later you need a graphic designer. Oh, if only you'd taken the business card of the person in line at the grocery store!

You will find potential resources through:

1. Networking – online and offline

2. Continuous learning

3. Sharing your vision with others. People will connect with it and show you how they can help.

Your resources are all around you. You simply have to recognize them and put them to good use. Don't neglect this very profitable and effective attribute of an entrepreneurial mindset. It'll help you with the attribute we talk about in the next chapter.

Chapter Seven

How to Wear the Entrepreneurial Hat (You're More Than a Manager)

Presumably you started your business for a number of reasons. Maybe you were inspired to make a positive change in the world. Maybe you wanted to share your knowledge, skills or experience with others.

Maybe you simply wanted to have the freedom to be your own boss and make your own decisions. Chances are you didn't want to become a "manager." Yet if you're spending your days managing:

- Email

- Customer service

- Fulfillment and delivery

- Bookkeeping

- Affiliates

- Autoresponders

- Project management

And much more, then you definitely don't have enough time to be an entrepreneur. You don't have the time you need to innovate, plan and take inspired action.

How to Wear the Entrepreneurial Hat

Presumably you won't be able to outsource, delegate and automate everything for your business. There will still be some managerial tasks you have to take on. There will still be many tasks you need to or want to handle that are not "entrepreneurial" in nature. It's your company and you're the person who gets to make the rule.

That being said it is very important to take the manager and task manager hat off on a regular basis and focus on being the entrepreneur. What does that mean? It means spending time brainstorming, innovating, creating and developing new business ideas and systems.

For example, the owner of a coaching business spends a lot of time actually coaching clients. It's still important to spend time to spend time each week creating systems, products and services that benefit their audience. They might create information products to generate passive income or brainstorm ways to offer more value to their coaching clients.

Here's how to make sure you consistently put on the "Entrepreneurial Hat."

Step One: Set Time Aside To Brainstorm and Plan

Planning is an important part of being a business owner. Consider setting time aside each week to plan your business. A bare minimum is once monthly. However, the more often you plan the more comfortable you'll be with the process.

Step Two: Delegate Responsibility

Outsourcing has already been mentioned. However, you can also partner, hire employees and embrace the idea of interns. Each new person you bring on your team plays an important role in your business. Let them play that role. Delegate responsibility so you have time to be the entrepreneur – so you have time to plan and grow your business.

Step Three: Know your Strengths and Weaknesses

We'll talk about this in Chapter Eleven but for now know that it's important when you're planning how to grow your business and profits that you're keenly aware of your strengths and weaknesses. This will help you plan your role in any new system, product or service you create. It'll also help you decide who to delegate or outsource tasks to.

It's important to acknowledge your role and responsibility for growing your business. That means setting time aside to make it happen. It also means knowing your strengths and weaknesses and then building a team of people to help you reach your goals. In order to do that you want to be able to share and communicate your vision.

Chapter Eight

How to Share Your Business Vision

Entrepreneurs are visionaries. They dream of the
possibilities and then take action to make it happen. That
means you want to be able to effectively communicate
your dream or vision. Here's how:

Create a Vision Statement

Do you have a vision statement? If not, spend some time
defining exactly what you want your business to become.

Your vision statement answers the question, "Where do I
want this business to go?" "What do I want this business
to be?"

Here's an example of a vision statement. "Five years from
now, my company will have annual revenues of over

$250,000 by consistently providing timely, reasonably priced repair and coaching services."

Of course the statement could have read to indicate a goal of reaching 1000 clients or broadening services to include information products. The vision statement is guided by you and what you want for your future and the future of your business. It doesn't have to be money focused.

If you don't have a vision for your business start creating it. Write it down and keep it somewhere handy. This will make it easier for you to access when you're making business decisions and it'll make it easier to communicate your vision.

Once you have a vision statement, the first step to communicating it is to be passionate about it. Are you excited about where your business is going and what the future has to offer?

So how do you consistently communicate your vision?

- Integrate it into your decision making process. For example, if you are presented with an opportunity ask yourself if it supports your vision.

- Find likeminded people through networking.

- Hire and work with likeminded people who understand your vision.

- Embrace your vision in your marketing and communications as well as your sales, fulfillment and customer service department – make it an integral part of your business.

Chapter Nine

How to Be a Problem Solver

The foundation of every business is that it solves a problem for their customers. It doesn't matter what business model or niche you're in as a business owner you are a problem solver. A personal trainer helps people solve the problem of their health and fitness. A cell phone store solves the problem of communication.

In order to grow your business you want to continue to identify the problems your audience and customers are experiencing and solve them with products, services and improved systems.

You are therefore a "problem solver." A problem solver is also an innovator – you come up with innovative solutions to problems. (Aka a Creative Problem Solver.)

One of the most difficult aspects of the "entrepreneurial mindset" is recognizing innovative opportunities and becoming a creative problem solver.

Peter Drucker, in his book "Innovation and Entrepreneurship, Practices and Principles," lists several potential sources for innovative opportunity including:

1. **Process Need**

   Process Need is the need for a solution arises from a process. For example, you're cutting an apple and you want an easier way to remove the skin. Ah-ha! The apple peeler is invented

2. **Industry Changes**

   Any new change to your industry provides new problems and new opportunities. Social media managers are an example of an industry created to solve the problem for an entirely new industry.

3. **Demographics**

As characteristics of the human population change so do the needs. For example, more self employed individuals means a demand for individual health insurance.

4. **Changes in Perception**

Perceptions change as cultures change. The "green" movement is a classic example of a change in perception. It has presented many new business opportunities and problems to solve. For example, "green" light bulbs.

5. **New Knowledge**

As we learn new things new needs and demands are created. For example, you learn that grape

seeds help with weight loss, suddenly there's a
need for grape seed extract and supplements.

Innovative opportunity is all around you. The trick is to
recognize it. Thinking about innovative opportunities
based on the above criteria may help you begin to develop
this skill.

Becoming an Innovator and Problem Solver

It's really a matter of recognizing opportunities and we've
already discussed how to accomplish that. Next, create a
process whereby you are able to document ideas as they
come to you. It may involve carrying around a small
notBook and pen (or it may involve simply dictating your
ideas into your phone or mobile device.

Create a habit of recording your ideas. The more you
record them as they come to you, the more ideas will
freely flow.

Chapter Ten

Entrepreneurial Mindset Means Being Willing To Take Risks

How much of a risk taker are you?
Chances are, if you own a business, you're at least willing to take some risk. Entrepreneurs aren't careless. They know the difference between apparent and actual risk. They take what's often called "calculated risk."

Calculated risk is risk that has been considered carefully. It's not without the potential for failure but you have carefully weighed the pros and the cons and decided to go ahead. The difference between an entrepreneur and most other people is that they're willing to take much more risk than others.

In fact, many entrepreneurs don't really consider the risks associated with failure or ridicule. These are two risks that stop most people in their tracks.

They're often not concerned about financial risk either. If you have a dream and you're passionate about it, the only risk to you is not seeing your dream become a reality – that's an entrepreneurial mindset.

Risk Assessment – What Are You Afraid Of?

Not all fears are created equal. Fearing for your life is much different than fearing ridicule.

The body has a similar adrenaline response but the actual outcomes are very different. Fear ridicule and you may miss out on owning your dream business. Fear for your life and you stay alive.

An entrepreneur assesses their fears from a place of logic. They ask themselves, "What do I really have to lose?"

Once you know the worst, you can prepare for the best. You can then set aside your fear or overcome it. Our logical minds can be both a hindrance and a help – the key is to use it to your advantage.

Embrace the entrepreneurial mindset and learn to recognize when your thoughts are limiting your success.

Speaking of learning…

Chapter Eleven

Entrepreneurs Always Learn and Improve

Entrepreneurs are motivated, right? We've already covered that. They're motivated to:

- Grow their business

- Make money

- Help people

- Work less and earn more

- Provide value

They're also motivated to learn, grow and improve themselves. Why?

Because self improvement and education helps them stay on the cutting edge of their business, offer more value to their customers, brainstorm and innovate new solutions, and ultimately make more money. Continued learning helps you also gain exposure to new people, thoughts, ideas, practices, philosophies, and opportunities.

Self improvement also helps you hone your entrepreneurial strengths. It helps you improve yourself. It also helps you adapt to new changes and opportunities quickly.

But how do you fit continued learning into your already busy life?

Create a goal, a plan and a strategy for success of course!

- Read blogs and industry magazines – use technology to deliver information to a reader or your email.

- Network online

- Join a mastermind group

- Attend classes, seminars and workshops

- Read industry books and business books

Consider the following goal – to attend one workshop, seminar or online class each quarter. Subscribe to 10 of the top industry blogs and read them weekly. Join a mastermind group or find a mentor/coach and to read one industry book each quarter.

Continued learning and self improvement also helps you increase your strengths and manage your weaknesses. Of course, first you need to know what they are. On to Chapter Twelve!

Chapter Twelve

Entrepreneurs Know Their Strengths and Weaknesses

Do you know what you're good at? Do you know where you need help in your business? This is truly important information. It takes a strong person to acknowledge their weaknesses and seek help for them.

For example, as a business owner maybe you're great at writing sales copy but not so skilled with the day to day content writing. Maybe your voice comes across as too salesy or forced and instead you want to be friendly and informative.

Instead of spending countless hours trying to improve your writing skills it might make more sense to find help in the form of a ghostwriter.

Entrepreneurs know that they cannot be good at everything and that it doesn't make sense for them to. Focus on your strengths. That's where the money and the satisfaction are. And find ways to manage or compensate for your weaknesses.

Hire experts. Create systems that don't require you to perform in your weak areas.

Improve your skills when and if it makes sense. For example if you want to be a better content writer or you simply cannot afford to hire someone to write all your content then it makes sense to work on improving your skills.

Sit down and document your strengths and weaknesses. Then create systems and solutions that work for you and your business goals.

Finally, because all work and no play really does lead to disaster, the next chapter takes a look at living a balanced life.

Chapter Thirteen

Entrepreneurs Live a Balanced Life

All work and no play is a surefire way to burn out, lose motivation and energy for your business. If you spend all of your time and energy building your business and don't spend any time on yourself, your friends, your family and the other aspects of your personal life you are in danger. There is the very real risk that you'll burn out, or worse – lose your personal life.

No one can tell you how to define success. You know what success means to you. And no one can tell you how to define a balanced life. You know what balance means to you.

Maybe balance means you work three weeks and then take a week off. Or balance might mean you work in the mornings and take the afternoons off. Or maybe the standard five day work week with two weeks' vacation is just fine.

The important thing to know is that you do need to take time off. You do need to focus on other things some times.

How do you know if you're living a balanced life? - It's pretty easy actually.

Do you wake up feeling motivated and enthusiastic about your day?
Are you able to focus on your tasks?
Do you feel creative and inspired?

If the answer is yes to all three then you're probably doing just fine. If you answer no to any of the questions at any time then you need a break.

Instead of waiting for that "no" answer and feelings of motivation to wane, plan for a balanced life. Schedule time off and figure out what you need both personally and professionally.

When you live a balanced life it's easy to unleash your inner entrepreneur. It's easy to embrace your entrepreneurial mindset.

Chapter Fourteen

A Positive Mindset and Productivity

You spend about a one-third of your life at work. If you're spending it with negative individuals, it may really affect you and bring you down.

By arresting negative thoughts as they enter your ears and not letting them go forward in your thoughts, you'll be doing a lot of the work to remain positive in a negative situation and build your business skills.

Here are ways to keep horrible situations at work from bogging you down:

Possess a life outside your job!

Keep acquaintances who have a good grasp of reality and with whom you are able to share life that's totally unrelated to the job you do. Refuse to even discuss your work outside work hours, particularly if the environment is toxic except when it comes to the ideas for your own business.

Recognize that most of what goes on at work and most of the negativism, even that directed at you, isn't about you!

Think about the stress your colleagues are facing at work, at home and in their personal lives and comprehend that they're projecting and displacing their angriness onto you and other people around them as well. Remember that dealing with people is crucial to being an entrepreneur.

Refuse to let your colleagues' workaholic, ambitions and selfish conduct seep into your system!

It's simple to start letting negative conduct creep in by agreeing with perspectives or taking sides. Rather, choose to rise above it all by staying neutral.
Defend your thoughts; they sooner or later become your reality!

Make certain the negativism around you doesn't continue playing in your head. Play music at your desk at a reasonable volume if you think it helps center you. Take breaks to collect your thoughts. Keep favorable reminders in quotes and pictures around your workspace about what you are trying to learn and accomplish.

Truly think about your options for beginning your entrepreneur journey!

A few bosses may be emotionally abusive; if the company surroundings don't look likely to change, evaluate whether this is truly the best place for you and ways you can start your own thing soon.

You spend eight plus hours a day at your desk juggling calls, e-mails and correspondences. All the same the stack of paper on your cluttered up desk continues growing taller, you eat more meals at the office than you do at home and you're still hardly meeting your deadlines.

Discover ways to keep away from time traps and to improve existing procedures to be not only more productive at work, but much less stressed and to develop skills that you can use in your own business.

Notice time wasters!

Standard culprits are instant messaging, net surfing, personal calls and gossip with colleagues. The minutes spent on these mis-directions may become hours of lost time and lost productivity. Determine limits on these actions and discover ways to politely end conversations!

Confine distractions and interruptions!

Schedule times to follow-up and respond to mail, e-mail and voice mail. If conceivable, switch off instant messenger programs and don't answer personal calls while you work at other tasks.

Coordinate and prioritize!

If you're consistently searching for items on your cluttered up desk, allow time to organize files, tools and equipment. Keep paper and electronic files in marked folders. On your PC, produce shortcuts and favorites to help find items rapidly and easily.

Utilize a single portable calendar to track all meetings, dates and deadlines!

Produce a schedule to begin and finish a given task and stick to it. Start and finish tasks on time. A daily or weekly "To Do" list may likewise be a helpful tool to stay on track and remain productive.

Be truthful with yourself about your fortes and failings and then budget time and jobs accordingly! It may be helpful to do the things that you like the least first, as they might be more time consuming and you're more likely to finish more interesting activities.

Compose agendas for meetings and remain inside the allotted time!

Inefficient meetings that go late are a huge cause of productivity loss. Put down all key information like date, time, attendees, schedule items and action items when taking notes. This might save considerable guessing later. When in doubt, document.

Learn to utilize new and better tools and utilize existing tools more efficiently. Discover a coach or mentor or take a class in time management, organizational strategies and productive business communication.

Take breaks!

This might seem conflicting when you are swamped. All the same, "crunch time" is when it's even more crucial to stay clear and centered. It's easy to make errors and when feeling deluged. Actually schedule breaks into your day if essential. Even a short walk around
the building may clear your head and bring down stress, which promotes productivity.

Chapter Fifteen

Learn To Listen to Customers!

Watch and learn from your people you work with because they frequently demonstrate the habits you'll need to have when you're living the life of an entrepreneur like how to listen to customers.

Notice What People Want!

There's a lot of discussion about listening these days. Listening is among the most crucial skills that you are able to learn. If you are able to really stop and listen to your customers, you are able to pave the path to ongoing business success.

Listening calls for paying attention and reacting to the needs and wants of customers. If you want to have your own business, you have to practice the art of active listening. It is not good enough to react to clients. You have to be able to anticipate their needs.

Listening to clients is about placing your company to be the answer to buyer needs, ideally previously them even asking. Listening is likewise about getting involved with your clients. This includes really spending time with them, exploring things that are significant to them, studying magazines and books that are written for them, and being an authority in the things that matter to them.

You're business ought to have an ideal customer. This is the prototype of the perfect client for you. You need to draw in this sort of client, and the more of your clients that fit the ideal, the better. So, it adds up that this is the sort of client you ought to be paying attention to.

A client is somebody who's purchased from you or the company you work for, but it's likewise somebody who may purchase from you. You ought to treat clients, prospects, and general public with equal respect. All the same, you ought to spend your time listening to the individuals who you most want as clients.

Listening may (and ought to) occur everyplace. That being stated, you are able to hone your listening by utilizing particular tools and strategies.

Offline, you ought to be conducting client surveys and just be getting out and talking to clients and people. Go to trade shows and conferences that are likewise attended by your ideal clients. If there are none in your area, begin one. As your expertness grows, you might want to think about doing a few speaking engagements. This is an awesome way to meet people and to get individuals to tell you about the problems that they face.

Online, the openings are endless. You are able to listen on Twitter with the help of Twitter Search. You are able to track key words and phrases across the net utilizing Google Alerts. Forums are a great place to listen. You are able to likewise produce your own listening posts with a blog or podcast. Sure, this is about you talking, but it will likewise force you to explore and learn about your clients. And you are able to encourage dialog and reader comments.

Make sure to listen where clients are talking! If you will be able to find out where ideal clients congregate, online and offline, then you have to be there too.

Active listening will help you to better comprehend and connect with your clients. It will make sales and marketing easier, as you'll be able to position yourself right between the client and the need.

Becoming a great listener will likewise endear you to the individuals you wish to reach. Everybody loves being listened to. So close that trap, put away that profit and loss sheet for a minute, and begin exploring the world of your clients.

Chapter Sixteen

Be A Good Provider!

We all supply value in the workplace—either by the work we inject as an employee, or with the products and services we sell in our business. A great performance review might not be enough to guarantee a promotion or even to keep your line of work. In addition to that, a high-quality product or service might not be enough on its own.

Give First Mentality!

Value is in the eye of the observer (think about how much more you may pay for an umbrella on a showery day). Workers who are simple to get along with and reliable with assignments will be more useful to their manager than somebody who produces stress in team meetings and on a regular basis misses deadlines.

In addition to that, a product will be more useful to a consumer if his or her favorite famous person endorses it, if it's on sale, or if it includes a contributed bonus. At the same time, we're becoming desensitized to ads; we've gotten to be wary of bonus offers, upsells and add-ons. We're seeking authenticity; that's what we value today.

Given the expanded rivalry in the job market, workers have to establish their value to the company in order to get and keep their lines of work, as well as to move ahead to higher positions and acquire customers when it comes to having the entrepreneur mindset. A lot of consumers are feeling whipped and worried and are guarding their buys cautiously. On the other hand, we're in the middle of a virtual flood of sales offers (no deficit there).

Consumers are picking out the products and service they perceive to be the most useful. You absolutely have to maximize the sensed value of what you offer. But you likewise need to support yourself and your loved ones. So what do you do?

Seek things you are able to add on to your products and services that won't cost you a great deal but are still really useful, e.g., a downloadable e-book or accompanying CD. Approach somebody who has a complimentary business that services your market, and ask him or her to chip in an additional product or service. It's a win-win, as they acquire the exposure to your clients or customers and you get the extra value for your offer.

Add to the sensed value of your product or service by including case studies and/or recommendations. Think about who may have the peak level of "societal capital" for your audience. Typically this will be somebody whom your leads may relate to as having like challenges and conditions OR somebody they look up to for having accomplished what they're attempting to accomplish.

Once you consider ways to amp up the sensed value of what you provide, put yourself in your customer's shoes. Is there something about your product or service that you brush aside, but that other people find useful? If you're not certain, survey satisfied buyers and customers.

Workers and business owners, make yourself essential to your team by demonstrating yourself as a connector. Listen for matters that individuals require and match them with individuals, products or services that have them. Naturally, do this for work projects and additional office tasks, but likewise extend it to personal issues. For instance, if somebody tells you about an awesome holiday spot, and somebody else is planning their next trip, suggest that the 2 individuals chat about it.

Point out the added value you're already giving to your customers!

Maybe you regularly catch clues that everybody else misses. Don't simply assume your clients will notice: point them out in an email or blog post!

In this crowded market, competitive business market and challenging economy, there are chances for the cream to rise to the top. Make certain you remind individuals of your value; why you're the cream as an entrepreneur.

Chapter Seventeen

Find A Mentor and Coaching!

A mentor is an individual with more experience in business, or merely in life, who may help an entrepreneur hone her or his powers and advise him or her on piloting fresh challenges.

A mentor may be a boon to an entrepreneur in a broad array of scenarios, whether they supply pointers on business technique, bolster your networking crusades or act as confidantes when your work-life balance becomes out of whack. However the first thing you need to know when seeking out a mentor is what you're seeking from the arrangement.

What having a personal trainer is to your body, having a coach may be to your mind. Utilizing a coach appears to be the latest way for some individuals to get ahead in today's gaga business world.

Learn From Others!

What may your mentor do for you? Ascertaining what type of resource you require is an imperative first step in the mentor hunt. Beginning with a list is a good opening. You might want somebody who's a great listener, somebody socially connected, somebody with expertise in, suppose, marketing, person accessible.

Ideally you may find a mentor with all of these characters, but the reality is you might have to make a few compromises. After you count the characters you're looking for in a mentor, split up that list into wants and needs.

The following step is to do an informational interview with many candidates and then go back to your standards that way you don't get blown away by chemistry and you remain centered on your business or personal reasons for needing a mentor. By judging a combination of the qualitative and quantitative properties of each of your likely
mentors, a prime candidate will come forth.

Bear in mind that it might be advantageous to have more than one mentor. If you think that you might monopolize too much of your mentor's time then several mentors might be the answer. The benefits of having multiple mentors is that you are able to get a lot of assorted viewpoints and when you have many mentors at a time, if they're seated around a table, the synergy between the mentors truly helps move your thinking along.

How to discover a mentor?

Begin with loved ones and friends - When seeking a mentor, begin close to home. Really close to home. Occasionally you are able to talk to your own relatives or friends, individuals who you trust, who you know, who you are able to sit and say: "Gee, what do you feel about this?"

Think about those in your broadened network - If your friends and loved ones provide you enough unsought advice already, and you don't believe that's the route for you, your left over options are individuals who don't know you as well or don't know you in the least yet.

How do you ask for such a huge commitment from a virtual stranger?

The opening move is to get hold of your network of contacts. A positive word from a common acquaintance may go a long way toward getting a mentoring relationship off to a great start. Additionally, you shouldn't pick out a mentor overnight, which implies you ought to keep your antenna poised to pick up on likely mentors at conferences, trade shows, and so forth. Meeting with a future mentor in person helps construct a rapport and you may wish to wait till that connection develops before tossing out the question.

Think about total strangers - perhaps none of the individuals in your network seem like a great fit for you. Begin doing a little research. Profiles of business owners in magazines and papers may key you in to somebody who equals your style. But when you have a few prospects go forward delicately.

Discover as much as you are able to about the likely mentor and attempt to schedule a brief interview by telephone saying you have a few particular questions or simply generally wish to pick their brain. You ought to travel to them and, particularly at first, make it as simple for them to help you as you are able to. At the end of your beginning interview, if it appears to have gone well, you may broach the idea of speaking once again, whether by telephone or in person, sometime in the time to come.

Over time, if they feel receptive, you may bring up the idea of a more conventional mentoring relationship with more particular parameters and goals.

Think about the rivalry - Well, not your direct rivalry. For instance, if you're in retail selling windsocks, somebody selling kites isn't in direct rivalry with you but may still have a few insights into the outdoor product industry. If you have a brick and mortar store, you may even call somebody who does precisely what you do in a far away location, suppose you're in New York City and they're in Arizona. However the web is increasingly placing retailers even on different continents in rivalry, so step lightly.

A different hint would be to seek out counsel from somebody at a business larger than yours who may be less likely to view you as rivalry. Tap your field - your suppliers, your local chamber of commerce, and relevant trade publishings are great sources for likely mentors.

These are all great places to come by knowledgeable individuals, but how do you find somebody who matches your personal flair? Look for a mentor the same way that individuals seek medical professionals, seek recommendations.

Pay for mentoring - But what if you have an awesome idea that you wish to get off the ground rapidly, and you need a fast jolt of expertise? Great informal mentorships are cultivated bit by bit and may frequently last for years. If what you require is a crash program, it may be time to bring in the consultants.

Individuals at all stages of professional evolution need coaches to help them. CEO's often utilize coaches to bounce ideas around, entrepreneurs utilize their coach to help them think strategically about the business, and coaches help other people sort out career decisions.

Think about the affect you are able to have by offering to coach your partners, employees and customers. You are able to be a coach to the individuals around you and help them to accomplish their goals faster and simpler.

Individuals seek coaches for 2 basic causes:

- A few individuals look for coaches to help them discover a balance between their
    personal and professional lives.

- Other people want coaches to help them get more productive in their business or help
    step-up their business.

Individuals aren't looking for speedy answers any longer. They're seeking ways to produce lasting change. The traditional consultant doesn't truly bring about lasting change. A coach is a sort of consultant who works with customers to come up with their own changes that are lasting.

Coaching is the next evolutionary stage of consulting. Coaching is a blend of business, finance, psychology, philosophy, transformation and spirituality. It helps individuals get more of what they wish out of life, whether it's business success, fiscal independence, academic excellence, personal success, physical wellness, relationships or career planning.

Coaches are soundboards, support systems, cheerleaders and teammates all rolled into one. Bottom line; the job of a coach is helping other people realize their total potential. Coaches utilize questioning skills, listening and motivational strategies to help individuals build the skills, knowledge and confidence required to better their professional and personal lives. A coach is a collaborative partner who helps you achieve things. Coaching isn't a replacement for personal responsibility and personal alteration or choice.

You require a coach if:

- Your business isn't performing as well as you wish.

- You feel you're working harder and are less gratified.

- Your business is doing well and you're getting sick of working so hard.

- A big downsizing in your company is causing big change in the work surroundings.

- You think your career is approaching a plateau.

- You got a subpar performance review.

- You're not able to mold and lead your staff.

- You're not easy making strategic conclusions.

A coach supplies you with a place to get a little perspective. A coach is somebody who isn't caught up in all the daily stuff and who may see the big picture.

About the Master-Mindset Method

● Do you know this urge from deep inside to make the best out of life?

● Do you know this hammering question in your mind if that's all what life can be?
   Or is there more to get, to achieve, to see, to live?

● Do you have ambitions, visions and dreams but it seems like just to be a silly
   daydream an never will become reality?

● Do you feel bored or frustrated sometimes because life is not what you wish and
   things just don't change?

→ Great!
   And I really do mean "great", because you are on the right track already.

Welcome to the Master-Mindset Method, a high effectively Self-Development System which combines the best knowledge and greatest techniques from many coaching styles like NLP, The Master-Key System or the Silva Mind Method. Combined with valid modern strategies from psychoanalysis or behavior therapy and ancient knowledge from Buddhism, Hinduism or the teachings of Hermes Tresmigistos, the Master-Mindset Method is all you need to succeed.

You don't need to read tons books and learn many different methods, because Stefan F.M. Dittrich, the creator of the Master-Mindset Method did so for you. He studied Personal- and Businesscoaching, is certified hypnotist, NLP-Trainer (DVNLP, IN), practical health-care instructor and much more. Also he is a Toastmaster degreed as Advanced Communicator Bronze and Advanced Leader Bronze. He worked in a German mental hospital for ten years and published several books. Also he is an active member of "Amnesty international" and "Being Human".

The Master-Mindset Method will take you by your hand and will show you step by step the way to transform your life from the actual situation into the life for which you had been incarnated. Therefor it's irrelevant if you want to grow rich, a great member of your family or society, if you want to realize the "unthinkable" or just want to be happy. The strategies and techniques from the Master-Mindset Method are universal usable and it's just up to you, what and who you want to become.

So get out of your comfort zone!
Because that is where magic happens.

Get up! Get out! Be awesome!

www.master-mindset.com

Because I think another important point for a successful Mindset is the deep desire to add value to the world by giving back and doing good things, I will give the floor to Ms. Sadika Kebbi, the chairwoman of "Kun Inssan" (Being Human), an awesome NGO I'm volunteering as ambassador, to use the last pages in this book to introduce the project:

The Story of the NGO "Kun Inssan" (Being Human)

It all started in 1975 when the Lebanese civil war took its toll and my childhood friend Jana was slaughtered at a Christian barricade.

Although ten years old, Jana and I did our best to look older with what we had – our clothing, and of course our mothers' make-up, accessories and high heels. We kept on laughing and crying our hearts out; we kept on smearing and cleaning our faces; we kept on wearing and removing our mothers' high heels, until the 6th of December 1975. It was black Saturday. Jana and her family left their house early on that cursed day and came back later that evening wrapped in spotted red and white sheets. My mother couldn't hold me from walking into Jana's bedroom. Her tiny body lied on a pink mattress. I couldn't cry on that day; instead I put the human within me to sleep and watched my small world shatter into eighteen sects. Rage, anger and hatred nibbled at my heart as media and adults determined my foes.

Two years later, my family and I took refuge at Uncle George's house, my father's childhood friend. A few hours later violent knocks shook the house's door. In a split of a second Uncle George was by my side; he took me in his arms and whispered into my ear; "No matter what happens don't look at the door; keep on reading this Bible; tonight your name is Mary." The door opens; "Good evening George; we heard that you are hiding some friends," said a muffled voice.

"You mean my brother Elie, his wife Anna and their two children Mary and Joseph; come in please let me introduce you." Another heart beat went by. I had never felt more afraid in my life then, "There is no need." At that moment, I took a peek and saw ten armed masked men leave Uncle George's doorstep. My world became confused, and I couldn't exclude Christians from my universe anymore. Uncle George awakened the hibernating human within me. He made me realize that no one can teach me hatred.

Growing up amidst the atrocities of war, the human within me kept on growing through sharing my story and listening to other people's stories; until I became to be known as the Storyteller who brings hearts together, speaks and listens to them, and thus "Kun Inssan" (Being Human) the NGO was born. One of "Kun Inssan's" purposes is to breach gaps among people from all walks of life through storytelling. It is an organization which will initiate change and bring peace by filling hearts with love.

"Kun Inssan" will be the first nomadic NGO to tour the world with a repertoire of stories in an attempt to create a community of storytellers from different cultural, religious, racial and ethnic backgrounds. One of its main targets is to create the first United Nations of storytellers for once hearts meet, speak and bond issues such as poverty, education, empowerment, development and health will have a better chance at being solved.

"Kun Inssan" or Being Human looks forward to grow its worldwide family through its ambassador Stefan Dittrich, as well as it looks forward to your support and efforts.